Anger management

Tactical approach to achieving temper control

Collin Theo

Table of contents

Chapter 1

Approaching anger

We all understand what anger is and have experienced it at some point, whether it was a little annoyance or a full-blown wrath. Anger is an entirely typical and typically positive human emotion. But when it spirals out of control and becomes destructive, it can cause issues—issues at work, issues in your personal relationships, issues with your life's general quality.

You may experience the feeling that you are at the mercy of a strong, erratic emotion when you are angry.
Anger, what is it?

What is fury like?

According to Charles Spielberger, PhD, a psychologist who specialises in the study of anger, anger is "an emotional state that ranges in intensity from mild irritation to severe fury and violence." Similar to other emotions, anger is accompanied by physiological and biological changes. For example, when you get angry, your blood pressure, heart rate, and levels of the hormones adrenaline and noradrenaline all increase.

Events both internal and external might trigger anger. A traffic delay, a flight cancellation, or a specific person or event could be the source of your rage, or it could be brought on by fretting or obsessing over personal issues. Angry feelings can also be brought on by memories of upsetting or painful experiences..

Fury is being shown

Responding violently is the automatic, natural manner that anger is expressed. Anger inspires strong, frequently aggressive sentiments and behaviours that enable us to fight and defend ourselves when we are attacked. Anger is a natural, adaptive response to dangers. Therefore, some level of rage is essential for our survival.

On the other hand, laws, cultural conventions, and common sense impose limitations on how far our anger can lead us. As a result, we can't physically lash out at every person or thing that frustrates or annoys us.

People deal with their anger feelings in a lot of conscious and unconscious means. The 3 key approaches are calm, inhibit, and express. The best way to cope with anger is to express it in a calm, non-aggressive manner. To do this, you must learn how to express your demands and how to meet them without causing harm to others. Accepting yourself and others means being forceful without being pushy or demanding.

Anger can be controlled, then transformed or directed. This arises when you suppress your rage, put it out of your mind, and concentrate on the good. Your anger is to be contained or suppressed in order to channel it into more useful activity. If your anger isn't permitted to find an outlet outside of yourself, it could move inward and toward you. Anger directed inward can result in hypertension, high blood pressure, and depression.

Anger that goes unspoken might lead to other issues. It can result in pathological outbursts of rage, such as passive-aggressive behaviour (assaulting others covertly without saying why rather than outright) or a constantly angry and cynical personality. People who constantly degrade others, criticise everything, and make cynical remarks lack the freedom to articulate their anger in order to feel better. They are prone to have many loving relationships, which is not odd.

You can now settle down internally. This involves controlling all your external actions and internal responses, slows your heart rate, easing yourself down, and letting the emotions pass.

"When none of these three strategies succeed, that's when someone—or something—is going to get wounded," observes Dr. Spielberger.

Anger Management

The goal of anger management is to reduce the physiological stimulation that anger creates along with your emotional feelings. You cannot change, avoid, or get rid of the things or people who irritate you, but you can learn to control your reactions.

Do you feel too angry?

There are psychological assessments that gauge how furious you feel, how easily you get upset, and how well you control your anger. But if you do have an anger management issue, chances are strong that you already know it. You may need

assistance learning more effective ways to deal with this emotion if you notice yourself acting in ways that seem terrifying and out of control.
Why are some people more angry than others?

Some people, according to Jerry Deffenbacher, PhD, a psychologist who specialises in anger management, are more "hot headed" than others; they become angry more easily and intensely than the average person. There are also those who are chronically irritable and grumpy but do not express their anger in loud and spectacular ways. People who are easily enraged do not always curse and throw things; they may withdraw socially, sulk, or to become physically ill.

People who are easily upset have what some 's referred to as a low tolerance for frustration, which means simply that they believe they should not be subjected to frustration, inconvenience, or annoyance. They can't take things in stride, and they're especially irritated if the situation appears unfair, such as being corrected for a minor error

Why are these individuals the way they are?

Many different things. An underlying factor could be genetic or physiological: There is proof that certain kids are naturally irritable, touchy, and quick to anger, and that these traits show themselves from a very young age. Sociocultural factors can be another. The expression of anger is frequently seen as undesirable; instead, we are taught that it is OK to express other emotions such as anxiety and melancholy. We don't learn how to manage it or use it in a positive way as a result.

Family history has been linked to behaviour, according to research. People who are easily offended typically originate from chaotic, dysfunctional households who struggle with emotional expression.

Is "letting it all hang out" a good thing?
This notion is currently seen as hazardous by psychologists. Some people abuse others using this theory as justification. According to research, expressing your anger outwardly just serves to fuel more hostility and aggressiveness rather than aiding you or the target of your rage in resolving the conflict.

It's essential to identify what makes you angry and then create coping mechanisms to prevent those triggers from sending you over the brink..

How to control your rage

Relaxation
Deep breathing and calming images are two straightforward relaxation techniques that can be used to reduce anger. You can learn relaxation techniques from books and workshops, and once you do, you can use those techniques whenever you need to. It might be a good idea for both of you to master these strategies if you are in a relationship with a hot-tempered partner.

You can attempt these easy steps:

Breathing from your chest won't help you relax; instead, take deep breaths from your diaphragm. Think of your "gut" as the source of your breath. Repeat calming verbs like "relax" or "take it easy" slowly. While taking a deep breath, say it aloud to

yourself. Use pictures to conjure up a tranquil moment from memory or your imagination. Slow, easy yoga-style movements might help you feel considerably calmer by relaxing your muscles.
Use these methods consistently. When you're in a stressful situation, get used to using them automatically..

Cognitive reorganisation

To put it simply, this entails altering your thought process. People who are angry often swear, use strong language, or otherwise express their feelings in these ways. Your thoughts can become too dramatic and overblown when you're furious. Replace these ideas with more sensible ones by trying. Say to yourself, "It's annoying, and it's understandable that I'm unhappy about it, but it's not the end of the world, and being angry is not going to cure it anyhow," as opposed to, "Oh, it's awful, it's terrible, everything's wrecked."

When referring to yourself or another person, use caution when using the words "never" or "always." Not only are statements like "this machine never works" or "you're always forgetting things" untrue, but they also give you the impression that your rage is well-founded and there is no hope for a solution. Additionally, they alienate and degrade individuals who might otherwise be eager to collaborate with you on a solution.

Remind yourself that getting angry is not going to fix anything, that it won't make you feel better (and may actually make you feel worse).

Logic fails because anger, even when it is justifiable, can easily degenerate into irrationality. So examine yourself using reason and reasoning. Remind yourself that the world is "not out to get you," and that you are merely going through some of the difficult times that come with daily living. Every time you feel your wrath getting the better of you, do this to help yourself gain a more objective viewpoint. People who are angry frequently make demands, such as fairness, appreciation, agreement, and a readiness to do things their way. People who are angry demand these things, and when their demands aren't met, their disappointment turns to anger. Everyone wants these things, and we are all hurt and disappointed when we don't get them.

People who really are furious need to transform their expectations into wants as part of their cognitive restructuring. They need to recognize their neediness. In other words, it's better to say, "I would like" rather than, "I demand" or "I must have." You won't feel angry when you can't receive what you want; instead, you'll feel frustration, disappointment, and hurt. Some individuals who are upset utilise their anger as a defence against being wounded, but this does not make the hurt go away.

Finding solutions

Sometimes the source of our fury and annoyance are the very real, inevitable obstacles in our lives. Although it typically acts as a good, natural response to these problems, anger is not always incorrect. The cultural assumption that every problem has a solution makes it much more upsetting when we discover that this isn't always the case. The best mindset to adopt in this situation is to focus less on finding a solution and more on how you approach and handle the problem.

Make a plan and keep track of your progress as you go. Make a commitment to doing your best but also resisting the need to berate yourself if you don't receive a response right away. You will be less likely to lose patience and fall victim to all-or-nothing thinking if you can approach the problem with your best intentions and efforts and sincerely try to tackle it head-on. Even if the problem is not remedied immediately.

Improved communication

People who are angry often leap to assumptions and take action on them, and some of those judgments can be quite wrong. If you find yourself in a heated argument, take a moment to compose yourself before responding. Slow down and give your words some thought rather than speaking the first thing that comes to mind. Take your time before responding while paying close attention to what the other person is saying.

Additionally, pay close attention to the cause of the anger. For instance, your "significant other" may prefer more intimacy and connection but you prefer a certain level of freedom. Do not portray your partner as a warden, jailer, or an albatross around your neck in retaliation if they start to condemn your behaviour.

Although it's normal to become defensive in the face of criticism, refrain from retaliating. Instead, pay attention to the message that lies underneath the words—that this individual can feel abandoned and unwanted. Don't let your anger—or your partner's—allow a conversation to spiral out of control. It might involve a lot of careful probing on your side and it might demand some breathing space. Keeping your composure will help you avoid a bad outcome.

With humour

In many instances, "silly humour" can help diffuse anger. One benefit is that it could enable you to gain a more impartial viewpoint. Think about what that term might actually seem like before you call someone a name or refer to them in an irrational way. Imagine a big sack of dirt (or an amoeba) sitting at your teammate's desk, chatting on the phone, and attending meetings, for example, if you think of your coworker as a "dirtbag" or a "single-cell living form" at work.
Every time you think of someone else's name, do this. Draw a representation of how the actual object could seem if you can. This will need a lot of work.

According to Dr. Deffenbacher, the underlying message of really furious people is "things oughta go my way!" People who are angry often believe that they are ethically correct, that any obstruction of their goals or changes to them are a terrible insult, and that they shouldn't have to go through this. Perhaps some others do, but not them!

Imagine yourself as a god or goddess, a supreme monarch who controls the streets, shops, and office space, walking alone and having the last say in every scenario while others bow to you, he advises, when you feel the impulse. You have a greater possibility of realising that perhaps you are being unreasonable and that the things you are furious over are actually not that essential the more specific your imagined situations might be.

Two warnings should be heeded while employing comedy. First, utilise humour to help yourself address your difficulties more effectively rather than merely trying to "laugh off" them.

Second, avoid using harsh, sarcastic humour; doing so is merely another harmful way to vent rage.

These methods have one thing in common: they encourage you to not take yourself too seriously. Although anger is a serious emotion, it frequently comes with thoughts that, when considered, are amusing.

Altering your surroundings

Our immediate environment might sometimes be the source of our annoyance and rage. You may feel burdened and resentful of the "trap" you seem to have fallen into as well as the individuals and things that make up that trap as a result of your problems and obligations.

Take a break for yourself. For moments of the day that you are aware are particularly stressful, make sure you have some "personal time" scheduled. One illustration is the working mother who has a standing rule that "nobody talks to Mom unless the house is on fire" for the first 15 minutes after she gets home from work. After this little period of aloneness, she feels more equipped to deal with her children's needs without losing her temper.

Some further advice for calming oneself down

Timing: If you and your partner frequently argue while discussing issues at night (perhaps because you're both sleepy, preoccupied, or it's just habit), consider switching up the times you discuss significant issues to prevent fights.

Avoidance: Shut the door if your child's disorganised room makes you angry every time you pass by. Don't force yourself to look at what infuriates you. Saying "Well, my child should tidy the room so I won't have to be furious" is not acceptable. The point is not that. The key is to maintain your composure.

Finding alternatives: If your daily commute through traffic makes you angry and frustrated, set a goal for yourself and learn or map out a different route that is less crowded or more beautiful. Or look for a different option, like a bus or commuter train.

Do you need therapy?

Consider counselling to acquire better coping strategies if you believe your anger is truly out of control, affecting your relationships and other significant aspects of your life. You can collaborate with a psychologist or other qualified mental health practitioner to create a variety of approaches for altering your thoughts and actions.

Inquire about their approach to anger management while speaking with a potential therapist, and let them know that you want to work on your anger issues. Verify that this isn't just a strategy meant to "bring you in touch with your sentiments and express them" because it may be the root of your issue.

According to psychologists, a person who is extremely furious can shift toward a median level of anger with counselling in 8 to 10 weeks, depending on the situation and the tactics employed.

What about a course on assertiveness?

It's true that people who are furious need to learn to be assertive (instead of aggressive), yet the majority of books and seminars on assertiveness development are geared toward those who don't experience enough rage. These folks prefer to let others walk all over them and are more meek and passive than the ordinary person. Most angry people don't react in that way. However, these books can offer some helpful strategies to apply in trying circumstances.

Remember, you can't get rid of rage, and doing so wouldn't be wise. Despite your best attempts, things will still happen that will irritate you, and occasionally that anger will be justified. Frustration, suffering, loss, and the erratic behaviour of others are inevitable parts of life. You can modify how these occurrences affect you, but you can't change the fact that they do. In the long term, you may avoid becoming even more miserable by learning to control your furious reactions.

FIND A PSYCHOLOGIST

Psychologists can assist individuals in identifying and avoiding the situations that make them furious. They can also offer advice on how to control the unavoidable rage that occasionally erupts without notice.
Youngster waving his fist on the street
What causes certain people to become more irrational when driving?

Risk-taking, angry, and aggressive thinking, as well as increased anxiety and impulsivity, are all characteristics of drivers who are more prone to experience road rage.

Symptoms of juvenile violence

Learn to see warning signals and regulate your anger before it gets out of control.

Anger
How to identify and manage rage

Anger is an unpleasant emotional state that is frequently accompanied by antagonistic thoughts, physical arousal, and unhelpful activities.
Managing your rage
Techniques for managing your rage: Managing one's wrath
Anger is a normal human emotion, and there are occasionally good reasons to be angry. However, unchecked rage may be detrimental
to your health and personal relationships. Thankfully, there are strategies you may learn to help you control your anger.

Chapter 2

Understanding your anger triggers

Understanding emotional triggers

Do you find it difficult to manage your wrath at times? Have you ever experienced an out-of-control outburst of wrath that lasted only a few seconds?
You can be referred to as "too sensitive" by others, or you might believe that others have a knack for setting off your triggers.
If any of these circumstances apply to you, you're definitely going through one of your emotional triggers.

What are anger triggers?

Like every other emotional response, anger has its triggers. It's a delicate section of your emotions that can be triggered by a certain circumstance, somebody, subject, etc.

No need for alarm. Everybody has emotional thresholds. Everybody experiences various emotions in different situations. What then produces these many triggers?

Your personal history makes a difference. Life experiences teach your brain how to respond in particular ways.

There are practically no limits to what can arouse an emotion. The list might go on and on and include a specific term, an action, a location, a person, etc. It's everything that your mind connects to a specific recollection from your past.

Understanding anger triggers

Triggers are challenging since you might not be aware of them. I frequently hear statements like, "I just lose control of my anger, but I don't know why," as an anger management counsellor in Denver. Your emotions are being activated in these circumstances without your knowledge.

Your triggers could include some apparent ones. You may be aware of the fact that you can become really irate depending on how your wife looks at you. Perhaps one of your children does something that really gets under your skin.

Determine what is causing your anger to flare up in the first step to changing your trigger. You will learn how to recognize and become more aware of your anger triggers through anger management treatment.

Being aware is the first step in providing effective therapy. Having things brought to your attention so you may modify how they affect your life is one of the most wonderful aspects of therapy. You have the power to manage your own emotions once you become aware of your anger triggers.

Managing anger's triggers

You can start to mend if you are more aware of what makes you angry. Anger triggers are frequently the outcome of emotional suffering. The job you must accomplish will be determined by the trigger.

For instance, your spouse can be the cause of your rage. You should probably think about how resentment is impacting your relationship in this situation. To alter your trigger for anger in this circumstance, you will need to practise forgiving others.

Working through some painful or unpleasant situations in your life is sometimes necessary to deal with anger triggers. When it comes to anger, common traumatic events include things like being abused as a child, being attacked, or being in a situation where your physical safety was in jeopardy.
Working through something such as a traumatic event or life experience might require some additional help from a mental health professional. If you find that you just can't seem to control your anger, you can find a qualified therapist in your area.

Anger Diary And Triggers

Man ratings help you to become conscious of your anger, but they won't help you stop being angry. In order to diffuse your anger before it gets out of control, you'll want to develop an anger plan listing out things you can do to calm yourself down.

For example, part of your plan might be to take a 'time-out' when you start getting upset; to temporarily remove yourself from the situation that is provoking you so as to provide yourself with a space in which to calm down. Another way to defuse anger might be to move the conversation away from what is bothering you and towards a more neutral topic.

There are lots of things you can do to defuse an angry situation once you start thinking about it. The best of them help you to effectively keep yourself calm without damaging your pride. As each person has unique strengths and weaknesses, each person's list of strategies for defusing anger will be slightly different.

Anger Diary.

Rage ratings help you understand just how angry you feel in certain situations, but they don't do much for predicting what situations are likely to set you off in the first place. "Prevention is the best medicine" as the saying goes. Being able to predict what situations will provoke you will be a tremendous aid in helping you keep your temper under control. You can choose to avoid provoking situations entirely, or, if that is not possible, you can prepare yourself with ways to minimise the danger of losing control prior to entering your dangerous situations.

An anger diary or journal can be a useful tool to help you track your experiences with anger. Make daily entries into your diary that document the situations you encounter that provoked you. In order to make the diary most useful, there are particular types of information you'll want to record for each provoking event:

What happened that gave you pain or made you feel stressed?
What was provocative about the situation?
What thoughts were going through your mind?

On a scale of 0-100 how angry did you feel? (Rage Rating)
What was the effect of your behaviour on you, on others?

Were you already nervous, tense, and pressured about something else? If so, what?

How did your body respond? Did you notice your heart racing, your palms sweating?

Did your head hurt?

Did you want to flee from the pressure or perhaps throw something?

Did you feel like screaming or did you notice that you were slamming doors or becoming sarcastic?

What did you actually do?

How did you feel immediately after the episode?

Did you feel differently later in the day or the next day?

What were the consequences of the incident?

After recording this information for a week or so, review your diary and look for recurring themes or "triggers" that make you mad. Triggers often fall into one of several categories, including:

Other people doing or not doing what you expect them to do

Situational events that get in your way, such as traffic jams, computer problems, ringing telephones, etc.

People taking advantage of you

Being angry and disappointed in yourself

A combination of any of the above

You'll also want to look for anger-triggering thoughts that reoccur again and again. You can recognize these particular thoughts because they will generally involve one or more of the following themes:

The perception that you have been victimised or harmed.

The belief that the person who provoked you meant you deliberately harm.

The belief that the OTHER person was wrong, that they should have behaved differently, that they were evil or stupid to harm you.

Use your anger diary to identify instances when you felt harm was done to you, why you thought the act was done deliberately, and why you thought that it was wrong. Tracking your thought patterns will help you begin to see the common themes in your experiences. Here are some examples of trigger thoughts to get you started:

People do not pay enough attention to your needs; they do not care about you.

People demand/expect too much of you.

People are rude or inconsiderate.

People take advantage or use you.

People are selfish; they think only of themselves.

People criticise, shame, or disrespect you.

People are cruel or mean.

People are incompetent or stupid.

People are thoughtless and irresponsible.

People do not help you.

People are lazy and refuse to do their share.

People try to control or manipulate you.

People cause you to have to wait.

And here is a list of situations where these themes are likely to occur:

When stating a difference of opinion

While receiving and expressing negative feelings
While dealing with someone who refuses to cooperate
While speaking about something that annoys you
While protesting a rip-off
When saying "No"
While responding to undeserved criticism
When asking for cooperation
While proposing an idea
At the base of all trigger thoughts is the notion that people are not behaving properly and that you have every right to be angry with them. Most people find a few thoughts that frequently trigger their anger. Look for instances of situations that trigger your anger and see if you can't identify the particular set of triggering thoughts that really do it for you.

The purpose of your diary is to help you identify patterns of behaviour and specific recurring elements that really "push your buttons". The more accurately you can observe your feelings and behaviours and the more detailed your anger diary, the more likely you will be able to identify anger triggers and how you react to them. Understanding the ways in which you experience anger can help you plan strategies to cope with your emotions in more productive ways.

Deactivating Your Triggers

Once you have identified some of your triggers and have begun to understand your trigger themes, you will be able to work more constructively to control your response to those triggers.

Anger-triggering thoughts occur automatically and almost instantaneously, so it will take some conscious work on your

part to identify them and to substitute something more to your liking.
For example, imagine you have just been cut off while driving on the freeway.
Take notice of the physiological anger signs that tell you you're upset. Take a deep breath, and try to look at the situation rationally instead of going with your first impulse to attack.
Instead of automatically assuming the driver that cut you off did it deliberately (which might be your first thought), consider the possibility that the other guy did not see you.
If you can consider that the provoking action was not aimed at you personally or was a mistake, it will be easier for you to tolerate.

When you feel justified in your anger, you are giving yourself permission to feel angry, whether or not it makes sense for you to feel that way. The faster you stop justifying your anger, the sooner it will begin to recede.

While all anger you feel is legitimate in that it is the reality of how you feel at a particular time, this does not mean that your choosing to act on your anger feelings is always justified.
Remember that being angry is quite bad for your health, and destructive towards your important relationships with others.

Chapter 3

Anger management techniques

What Is Anger Management Therapy?

Anger is a normal human emotion that most people experience every now and then. However, if you find yourself feeling angry very often or very intensely, it may start to become a problem.

"Rage, persistent anger, or angry outbursts can have detrimental consequences for physical health, quality of life, and relationships," says Erin Engle, PsyD, a psychologist at Columbia University Medical Center.

"Anger management is an approach designed to help you manage the emotional and physiological arousal that accompanies anger. As it's often not possible to change the circumstances or people that elicit anger, anger management can help you recognize your triggers for anger and learn to cope with them more effectively," explains Engle.

The aim of anger management therapy is to help minimise stressful or anger-evoking situations, improve self-control, and help you express your feelings in a healthy manner, according to Engle.

Types of Anger Management Therapy

These are some of the different approaches to anger management therapy:

Cognitive Behavioral Therapy (CBT): CBT is often the treatment of choice for anger management, according to Engle. She says it can help you understand your triggers for anger, develop and practise coping skills, and think, feel, and behave differently in response to anger, so you are calmer and more in control.

Dialectical Behavioral Therapy (DBT): According to Engle, DBT is a form of CBT that can help individuals with intense or frequent anger regain emotional control through developing emotional regulation and distress tolerance skills, mindfulness, and effective communication in relationships.

Family Therapy: This form of therapy can be helpful in situations where anger is often directed at family members. It can help you work together to improve communication and resolve issues.

Psychodynamic Therapy: Psychodynamic therapy can help you examine the psychological roots of your anger and your response to it, so that you can identify and correct unhealthy patterns.

Your mental healthcare provider will evaluate your circumstances and specific behaviours to determine the overall approach to treatment and whether you require medication in addition to therapy, says Engle.

Technique

Anger management therapy techniques can involve understanding your triggers and responses to anger, learning strategies to manage or diffuse it, and changing thoughts and attitudes related to anger. Engle outlines some of these techniques below.

Identifying Triggers and Responses

Therapy can help you develop a better understanding of the factors that contribute to expressions of anger; current and past triggers for anger; your responses to it; and the consequences or aftereffects to yourself and your relationships.

For instance, you may realise that yelling at your spouse is related to observing your parents yell, or the belief that you'll only get what you want if you yell.

Learning Strategies to Diffuse Anger

Anger management therapy can equip you with strategies to disrupt your anger or manage your response to it through avoidance or distraction.

Your therapist can help you problem-solve how to respond when you’re angry. Role-plays offer opportunities to practise skills such as assertiveness and direct communication that can enhance control.

Therapy can also teach you coping strategies and relaxation techniques, such as slow deep breathing, leaving the room and returning when you're collected, or using a relaxing image to alleviate the intensity of anger.

Changing Attitude and Thought Patterns

Therapy can also involve restructuring thinking and changing attitudes related to anger, particularly if your therapist is taking a CBT approach.

Your therapist will help you examine your attitudes and ways of thinking and help identify patterns such as ruminating, catastrophizing, judging, fortune-telling, or magnifying that might exacerbate anger.

Your therapist will also work with you to help you practice changing your response patterns. They can encourage forgiveness and compassion, offer ways to let go of hurt and disappointment, and help you repair and accept ruptured relationships.

While anger management is a form of treatment designed to help you manage anger, anger is not officially a condition that is diagnosed or defined, like depression or anxiety, for instance. However, intense, destructive, or uncontrollable anger may cause significant distress and impairment and impact safety, says Engle.

Anger management therapy can help anyone who experiences rage or has angry outbursts. Anger management therapy can help improve your:

Mental health: Anger can consume your focus, cloud your judgement, and deplete your energy. It can also lead to other mental health conditions such as depression and substance abuse.
Physical health: Anger manifests physically in the body with a surge of adrenaline, a rapid rise in heartbeat, higher blood

pressure, and increased muscle tension in the form of a clenched jaw or fisted hands, says Engle. Over time, this can take a toll on your health and lead to physical health conditions

Career: Anger can make it hard for you to focus on school or work and affect your performance. It can also harm your relationships with your peers. While creative differences, constructive criticism, and healthy debates can be productive, lashing out or having angry outbursts can alienate your peers and lead to negative consequences.
Relationships: Anger often harms loved ones the most and can take a toll on your relationships with them. It can make it difficult for them to be comfortable around you, erode their trust and respect, and be especially damaging to children.

Anger management therapy is sometimes court-ordered in case a person has committed criminal offences, such as:

Assault
Battery
Disturbing the peace
Domestic abuse or violence
Rape

The Effects of Poorly Managed Anger
Benefits of Anger Management Therapy
These are some of the benefits anger management therapy can offer:

Identify triggers: Knowing what situations trigger your anger can help you avoid them or manage your reaction to them.

Change your thinking: Anger management can help you identify and change unhealthy thought patterns that fuel your anger.

Develop coping skills: Therapy can help you regulate your emotions, control your actions, and develop skills to help you cope with situations that trigger your anger.

Learn relaxation techniques: Your therapist may teach you relaxation techniques that can help you calm yourself down and relax your body and mind.
Solve problems: If certain situations trigger your anger repeatedly, your therapist may encourage you to look for solutions or alternatives.

Improve communication: Anger management therapy can help you express your feelings in a healthy, respectful, or assertive manner, without being aggressive.

How to Deal With Your Anger effectively

According to Engle, CBT, which is often used to treat anger, is a very effective approach. CBT is an empirically-supported treatment that takes a skills-based approach to anger management, with emphasis placed on awareness of thoughts, behavioural patterns, and skill development with respect to physical and emotional reactions to anger, says Engle.

A 2017 study found that CBT was helpful to table tennis players with anger management issues. Even one year after completing treatment, participants were less likely to negatively express anger or react angrily.

A 2020 study found that anger management therapy was beneficial to patients with HIV.2

Things to Consider

"As with any form of treatment, it can be beneficial to seek out the support and experience of a trained mental health professional. Professional evaluation and consultation can help identify any co-occurring mental health issues like trauma or substance use," says Engle.

If you have a co-occurring mental health issue, it may be beneficial for you and your mental healthcare provider to determine if those disorders play a predominant role or how they can best be addressed in combination with anger management, according to Engle.

Depending on your co-occurring issues, your mental healthcare provider will determine an appropriate treatment plan and whether or not you require medication, explains Engle.

How to Get Started

If you find yourself arguing often, becoming violent or breaking things, threatening others, or getting arrested because of incidents related to your anger, you may need to seek anger management therapy.

Look for a trained mental health professional who specialises in this form of treatment.

Depending on your preferences, you can choose to opt for individual treatment or group therapy. Individual therapy sessions offer more privacy and one-on-one interaction whereas group therapy sessions can help you feel like you're not going through this alone.

A Word From Verywell

Anger is a universal emotion that often arises in response to threat, loss of power, or injustice, says Engle. She explains that anger is not necessarily negative, though it can be detrimental at uncontrollable levels, given the behaviours likely to follow anger such as throwing things, walking out, attacking others, saying things you later regret, or acting passive-aggressively.

Anger can take a toll on your health, relationships, and career. Anger management therapy can help you regulate your emotions, maintain self-control, develop coping strategies, and communicate effectively.

Chapter 4

Turning anger to creativity energy

Befriending your dark emotions can empower your creative side
We all know anger, that fiery tornado that stirs up the belly or the base, storming through the heart and throat, demanding a voice... but what do you do with your anger? What is your relationship with anger? Is it the disowned and dishevelled mad relative you lock in the attic; the itinerant toddler you bundle out of sight, or the problematic and difficult person you patronisingly and with lying snow calm, ignore?

Perhaps you are so disconnected from anger, you have no idea the rumbling of the volcano in your tummy is even happening. You may be floating around in a disembodied sea of fake smiles and jittery mental dreaminess.

Anger is either repressed or expressed. Repression is a denial of reality. We shove down the powerful anger flooding our entire body, pretending it's not there. Anything repressed goes underground where it turns into a poisonous autocrat lurking ominously, waiting for an opportunity to break out.

Anger is an acid that can do more harm to the vessel in which it is stored than to anything on which it is poured. –
Anger is our Friend
Repressed anger tends to become uncontrollable and explosive. It is unpredictable and a force to be reckoned with. So often

inner restlessness is a volcano of repressed emotions. Even more destructive can be the alternative: the raging expression of anger and the dumping of our emotions on someone else like an out of control road train. This can be disastrous for our relationships and our health.

Accepting and acknowledging anger goes a long way to defusing the charge behind it. Too many of us were admonished to stop being angry as young children and teens. As a small child I remember my grandmother standing over my little brother and telling him she'd beat his temper out of him. Indeed a strange but probably not untypical way of dealing with a two or three year olds' temper tantrums.

So how do we deal with this "rogue" emotion anger?

Anger has been given a bad rap. It is so often maligned as a negative, destructive force that causes huge problems. Certainly when unleashed on others inappropriately it can scar relationships and be a raging fire destroying everything in its path. We would be lying most politically if we claimed to be spiritual and without anger! So how do we express anger not only constructively, but also creatively

Sloth, apathy and despair are the enemy. Anger is not. Anger is our friend. Not a nice Friend. Not a gentle friend. But a very, very loyal friend. It will always tell us when we have been betrayed. It will always tell us when we have betrayed ourselves. It will always tell us that it is time to act in our own best interests. Anger is not the action itself. It is action's invitation to action.

Acceptance

A willingness to face our subconscious mind with loving compassion and meet ourselves in our "darkest" expression is helpful in taking the sting out of anger. Instead of denying this natural force and fighting a part of ourselves, when we welcome and channel it with awareness, we awaken disowned parts of ourselves. By accepting anger as a natural and necessary force of creation, we can use it wisely and like the rider steering the horse, let it take us somewhere beautiful.

Acceptance is the acknowledgement that we are feeling anger. It is being open and non-judging, aware that anger is energy in motion, and that it is a messenger. The simple action of welcoming anger releases the possibility for anger to open the doorway to vitality, creativity and wisdom.

Anger or hatred is like a fisherman's hook. It is very important for us to ensure that we are not caught by it. –

LEARNING TO ACCEPT OUR SHADOW SIDE

Listening to the message

By bringing awareness to the anger we're feeling, throwing the door open, welcoming and making it a cup of tea, then sitting down in your kitchen together, you significantly alter and defuse the diabolical force of disowned anger. Anger is an emissary. Anger comes as an agent of change with a message for you. It brings letters informing you what's not working, is broken, needs updating, or is not serving you. If you listen with awareness, it shows you the map to freedom ... the pathway to living an authentic life. Anger is a signpost, signalling where you're off course.

Owning your anger leads to power

As you give yourself permission to freely express anger masterfully, you begin to unlock your power. You become potent, expressive, passionate and alive. Anger is life flowing through you telling you what you need. So many young girls were given the message that anger is not feminine, and is ugly. Today so many women carry a legacy of repressed, disowned anger, which renders them impotent and saps the potential of their power and leadership.

Unlocking anger and expressing it masterfully is one of the keys to your power. As you let this force live within you, you open the potential of the universe to flow through you unhindered in wonderful ways. A real boon for creative expression.

Expressing emotions through art is not something new, it's as old as creativity itself. But I think there can be an upgrade to the quality of expression, moving from the violence of Van Gogh's ear episode or other tortured artists, to the channeling of anger as impersonal energy, a force in and of itself, Kali-esque burning through the undergrowth. A journey of discovery, an acceptance of what is present and a fiercely authentic expression of this energy.

By journeying with and through anger, we discover a deeper, richer place within us, a wellspring of creative potential. Much like the process of Gabrielle Roth's Five Rhythms, surrendering to anger in a soulful, intimate dance practice of being with ourselves, leads to lyrical beauty and inner peace. I've had times where I've turned to my keyboard in desperate anger, not hammering out Beethoven, but releasing a vibrant passion through my arms and fingers that always becomes a delightful and surprising intimacy with my inner world. We can use the energy of anger itself, to burn the anger out and find compassion and peace.

CHANNELLING ANGER INTO CREATIVE EXPRESSION
When we give anger permission and freedom to be there, and listen to its message, we can transform what is holding us back, make the changes that get us back on track and serve our higher purpose, and also become aware of the deep pain that is often living beneath anger.

Anger and Passion

Atira Tan, the Founder and Executive Director of the Art2Healing Project, working to save and support children who have been the
victims of sex trafficking in Asia, shares how she deals with anger at the tremendous abuse she witnesses: “I used to be angry with the sex traffickers for what they did to the children, then the more I worked to stop this terrible industry, the more I developed compassion for them too. The anger became an intense determination to work harder to break the cycle and change lives.”

The way to change others’ minds is with affection and not anger.

LEARNING HOW TO TURN ANGER INTO CREATIVITY THAT CAN CHANGE THE WORLD

Anger and passion stem from the same source in the body. Anger is a really passionate life force trying to express itself through you. Anger can be suppressed by creativity wanting an outlet, but shoved aside due to the responsibilities of daily life.

Next time you're angry, meet yourself, with acceptance, awareness, feel the energy of the anger and use this energy to create something. Aware anger can change the world.

Martin Luther King, Aung San Suu Kyi, Gandhi, and Nelson Mandela, all used the inner message of anger to create transformation. In their mastery of anger walking the path with it as an ally, they unleashed tremendous creativity to achieve their ends, mobilising others and ultimately making an incredible mark on humanity. Their artistry of anger changed the lives of many forever.

How To Turn Anger Into Creative Energy?

Everyone gets angry now and then. Here's how to put it to good use.
Most of us recognize that you have to fail on the road to success. We know learning from mistakes is what perseverance is all about. But if that's true, then the emotions those setbacks unleash are also key ingredients in that process.

There's no point tip-toeing around the fact that everyone gets fed up from time to time. But neurological research hints that anger might lay the groundwork for creativity and can be harnessed to solve problems.

WHAT HAPPENS WHEN WE GET ANGRY

First, a quick primer on the physiology of anger. Emotions surface because our brains use memories and past experiences to determine the severity of a situation. If it's similar to something bad we've gone through before, we experience negative feelings as a way of protecting us from being hurt again and remembering that situation for future reference.

Unfamiliar and highly emotional experiences cause different patterns of neurological activity in our brains than when we feel calm and secure. The hypothalamus triggers the release of stress hormones, and the sympathetic nervous system flips into "fight or flight" mode as adrenaline and cortisol begin pumping through the body.

HOW CREATIVITY WORKS

Steve Jobs believed that "creativity is just connecting things." In 1998, he told Wired magazine that someone is creative because they "were able to connect experiences they've had and synthesise new things. And the reason they were able to do that was that they've had more experiences or they have thought more about their experiences than other people."

In other words, we generate new ideas when we can connect past experiences to something that's happening in the present in order to piece together a new solution—almost like a puzzle.

HOW TO PUT ANGER TO USE

Being angry typically makes us act irrationally and unpredictably. We imagine doing things we never actually follow through with. Yet we're so emotionally heated that we give short shrift to the social standards that otherwise manage our thoughts, behaviours, and decisions.

Those are pretty good conditions for creative thinking. Not only are our memories pushed to the surface, but our imaginations are running in overdrive and we're pushing past the usual thresholds for what we consider possible.

Here are three steps to unlocking your creativity when you're angry:

1. Find an activity that takes you away from what's making you angry and lets you release it. Exercise is a common outlet, but anything that distracts your mind through a form of physical movement can work well, from a brisk walk to an interactive video game. You can even try writing by hand as a last resort. Personally, I prefer running to blow off steam.

2. Embrace the anger and use it to push yourself harder. Do this for the first 10 to 20 minutes. Don't try to think positively yet. Run faster, punch harder—just keep moving. You'll probably find you can get into "the zone" much more easily when you're angry. Endorphins will begin to flood into your system, and you'll gradually begin feeling better and thinking more clearly.

3. Start thinking about things you want to do differently and problems you want to solve. This is the period when creativity really begins to soar. Don't force it, but while you're doing your chosen activity, focus on some of those obstacles and ambitions. Maybe it's a new project, a habit change, a career move, a trip you really want to take, or a new business idea. Maybe it's even the issue that got you mad in the first place.

It's important not to push yourself too hard mentally while you're pushing yourself physically. Just try to let the ideas flow as your mind begins to clear. If you can't think of anything, don't stress yourself out. The main thing is you'll get better at connecting and synthesising experiences over time so the next time something angers you, you'll be more prepared to tap into it creatively.

www.ingramcontent.com/pod-product-compliance
Lightning Source LLC
LaVergne TN
LVHW020532160826
845677LV00015B/4017

* 9 7 9 8 3 6 7 4 4 3 7 2 1 *